# HOW TO PLAY GUITAR FOR BEGINNERS

Discover Pro Tips, Learn Essential Techniques, Chords, Rhythms, Soloing Tips, Tunings, Improvise Like A Pro, And Build Your Repertoire From Scratch

## MYLA PRESLEY

# CONTENTS

## CHAPTER ONE ..............................................10

### Overview Of The Lap Steel Guitar .........10

### A Comprehension Of The Lap Steel Guitar ..........................................................10

### Introduction To The Lap Steel Guitar ....12

### Hardware And Accessories Required To Play The Lap Steel Guitar ......................15

## CHAPTER TWO ..............................................20

### Maintenance On A Lap Steel Guitar ......20

### Engaging In Open Chords .....................23

### An Examination Of Major And Minor Scales ..................................................25

### An Overview Of Slide Techniques .........26

## CHAPTER THREE ..........................................30

### The Integration Of Vibrato And Expression ............................................30

### Acquiring Fundamental Licks And Riffs .32

### Comprehending Timing And Rhythm ....34

Utilizing Backing Tracks For Practice .....36

CHAPTER FOUR .........................................40

An Overview Of Various Styles, Including Blues, Country, Hawaiian, And Others ..40

Suggestions For Enhancing Your Playing ....................................................................43

Preserving The Lap Steel Guitar ............45

Conclusion .............................................47

Copyright © 2024, Myla Presley

All Rights Reserved

No part of this book may be reproduced, distributed, or transmitted in any form or by any means, including photocopying, recording, or other electronic or mechanical methods, without the prior written permission of the author, except in the case of brief quotations embodied in critical reviews and certain other noncommercial uses permitted by copyright law.

## DISCLAIMER

The information provided in this book, is for general informational purposes only. The author and publisher make no representations or warranties of any kind, express or implied, about the completeness, accuracy, reliability, suitability, or availability with respect to the content contained herein.

Any mention of individuals, products, websites, organizations, or other names is purely for informational purposes and does not imply endorsement or affiliation.

The author and publisher do not endorse, recommend, or promote any specific individuals, products, services, websites, organizations, or other entities mentioned in this book.

All efforts have been made to ensure the accuracy and reliability of the information presented. However, readers should also consult with qualified professionals or instructors for personalized guidance and instruction.

Readers are advised to use their discretion and seek professional advice or guidance where appropriate.

The author and publisher shall not be held liable for any loss, injury, or damage arising from the use of information presented in this book.

By reading this book, readers acknowledge and agree to the terms of this disclaimer.

# ABOUT THIS BOOK

For individuals embarking on the journey of lap steel guitar playing, "How to Play Lap Steel Guitar for Beginners" functions as an indispensable manual. This book commences with an extensive introduction that establishes the groundwork for comprehending the intricacies of this distinctive instrument. The subsequent section instructs the reader on how to begin playing their lap steel guitar, detailing the necessary accessories and equipment to ensure a satisfactory experience.

A key topic addressed in this book is tuning, which guarantees that novices commence their musical journey on the appropriate pitch and cultivate a keen sense of pitch. The comprehensive elucidation of fundamental techniques and hand positioning establishes a firm foundation for proficiently investigating major and minor scales while performing open chords.

By introducing slide techniques, students are allowed to enhance their learning experience by incorporating expressive and vibrato elements into their playing style.

Beyond fundamental concepts, this book explores more complex subjects, including the acquisition of fundamental melodies and riffs, comprehension of rhythm and timing, and the utilization of accompaniment recordings for practical application to augment musicality. In addition, various playing genres such as country, Hawaiian, and blues are introduced, providing readers with a comprehensive comprehension of the lap steel guitar's versatility.

This book provides insightful advice on how to enhance one's playing abilities and provides comprehensive instructions on how to properly maintain a lap steel guitar to ensure its optimal performance and longevity.

"How to Play Lap Steel Guitar for Beginners" is an essential resource for individuals aspiring to become lap steel guitarists due to its comprehensive approach. It offers a methodical and user-friendly course that facilitates the mastery of this captivating instrument.

# CHAPTER ONE

## Overview Of The Lap Steel Guitar

For novices, learning to play lap steel guitar can be an exhilarating endeavor. Leaning towards the mesmerizing tones of blues, the country twang, or Hawaiian silky tones, the lap steel guitar provides a distinctive and adaptable musical encounter. This instructional manual will cover the essential aspects of lap steel guitar playing, commencing with an introduction to the instrument and progressing to the execution of a few basic notes. Upon completion, you will possess a strong basis upon which to further develop your expertise in lap steel guitar.

## A Comprehension Of The Lap Steel Guitar

Before beginning to perform, it is vital that you become acquainted with the lap steel guitar and its distinctive qualities. In contrast to conventional guitars, lap steel guitars are performed in a horizontal position, either on the lap or a raised surface, such as a table or stand. By arranging the strings in this manner, effortless entry is achieved, which further enables the implementation of a metal slide or bar to generate unique sliding noises.

The lack of frets is one of the defining characteristics of the lap steel guitar. As an alternative to forcing strings against frets to generate distinct melodies, musicians employ the slide to manipulate the length of the vibrating segment of the strings, thereby causing an alteration in pitch. The execution of slide guitar playing necessitates dexterity and supervision to accomplish seamless transitions between musical notes.

There are lap steel guitars available in variations with fewer or more strings than the standard six. They are frequently tuned to open tunings, which produce chords when the strings are strung without pressing down on any fret. Among the frequently used open tunings for lap steel guitars are Open D (D-A-D-F#-A-D) and Open G (D-G-D-G-B-D).

Lap steel guitarists may strike the strings with fingerpicks or their bare fingertips, in addition to the slide, to generate an assortment of tones and textures. By experimenting with various plucking techniques, one can cultivate an individualized playing manner and sound.

## Introduction To The Lap Steel Guitar

It is time to begin playing the lap steel guitar now that you have a fundamental understanding of the instrument. The following stages will assist you in commencing your journey:

1. Tuning Your Guitar: You must calibrate your lap steel guitar to the intended tuning before you can begin performing. Consider utilizing a tuner app or electronic tuner to ensure precision if you are new to tuning.

It is imperative to tune every string to its designated pitch by the tuning selected.

2. Establishing a Comfortable Seating Position: Position your lap steel instrument on a raised surface or on your lap, ensuring that it is level. Ensure that the instrument is positioned at a height that facilitates easy access to the strings and that it is stable. Investigate various seating configurations until you identify one that is both ergonomic and conducive to playing naturally.

3. Acquiring Foundational Techniques: Commence by acquainting oneself with fundamental slide techniques, which encompass the seamless transition between notes and the consistent application of pressure to the strings. Engage in deliberate practice by employing the slide to perform scales, simple melodies, and chord progressions. Explore diverse patterns and dynamics to cultivate your command and expressiveness.

4. The development of finger strength is a crucial aspect of lap steel guitar playing, particularly when utilizing the slide. As your proficiency develops, integrate finger-strengthening exercises into your routine, such as honing scales and arpeggios. Gradually escalate the difficulty and velocity as your abilities progress.

5. Investigating Resources: Employ digital tutorials, instructional videos, and literature specifically devoted to the art of lap steel guitar performance. As you advance, the guidance provided by these resources regarding technique, theory, and repertoire will assist you in expanding your knowledge and abilities.

6. Experimenting with Sound: As your proficiency with the fundamentals increases, feel free to explore various tunings, techniques, and effects to generate distinctive noises and styles that are uniquely yours. Unleash your creative inquisitiveness and artistic inclination

towards diverse musical genres, such as the gritty blues of the Mississippi Delta or the effortless sway of Hawaiian music, to cultivate your musical style as a lap steel guitarist.

Through a commitment to practicing and experimenting with these foundational principles, novices can tap into the creative capabilities of the lap steel guitar and commence a gratifying musical expedition. By exercising perseverance, demonstrating patience, and adopting an exploratory mindset, one can rapidly transform their music into something mesmerizing, imbued with the emotive allure of the lap steel guitar.

## Hardware And Accessories Required To Play The Lap Steel Guitar

In addition to skill and dedication, lap steel guitar playing also necessitates the utilization of appropriate equipment and accessories that augment the musical encounter. Whether you are an experienced player or a novice, possessing the proper equipment can have a substantial impact on your comfort and sound quality. Assemble the essential equipment and supplementary items required to play lap steel guitar.

It is essential to begin by acquiring a lap steel instrument. Lap steel guitars, in contrast to conventional guitars, are operated horizontally across the practitioner's lap, with the notes being fretted using a slide bar. To determine which lap steel guitar to purchase, one should take into account construction quality, scale length, and tonal characteristics. Begin users may choose to begin with more economical models and subsequently upgrade as their proficiency and personal preferences develop.

The slide bar is an essential accessory for lap steel guitar performance. Placing it on the finger, this cylindrical or tubular instrument is utilized to fret the strings by gliding along the notes. Typical materials used to construct slides include ceramic, metal, and glass, each of which imparts a distinct tone and feel. Glass slides may be more manageable for novices, whereas metal slides produce a more vibrant effect.

Furthermore, it is critical to acquire a high-quality amplifier to attain the intended volume and sound quality. The sustained and distinctively silky tone produced by lap steel guitars is enhanced by amplification. Consider purchasing an amplifier with tone-shaping controls and built-in effects so that you can customize the sound to your preference.

To maintain the tuning of your lap steel guitar, a dependable tuner is an absolute necessity. Electronic tuners offer precise tuning guidance and are user-friendly, enabling individuals to sustain intonation that is precisely on the pitch throughout rehearsals and live performances.

The following additional accessories may further improve your lap steel guitar playing experience:

• Picks: Although lap steel guitars do not typically utilize traditional guitar picks, fingerpicks can be utilized to achieve a more precise and rapid plucking of the strings.

• Concert bag or case: A padded concert bag or rigid case will safeguard your lap steel guitar during transport and storage.

• A perch or stand that can be adjusted: Ensuring a suitable playing posture is of utmost importance when engaging in prolonged lap steel guitar sessions. Utilizing an adjustable stand or seat can assist in determining the ideal height and angle for playing.

• Strings: To preserve the tone and functionality of your lap steel guitar, it is vital to replace the strings regularly. Determine which string material and gauge correspond to your playing technique in terms of tension and resonance by conducting experiments.

By procuring the necessary equipment and accessories, one will possess the necessary readiness to commence the pursuit of lap steel guitar mastery with assurance and eagerness.

# CHAPTER TWO

## Maintenance On A Lap Steel Guitar

Assembling a lap steel guitar for performance entails the most fundamental tuning. In contrast to the conventional tuning of standard guitars, which proceeds from lowest to highest pitch, lap steel guitars are frequently tuned to open tunings, thereby facilitating the execution of slide melodies and chord voicings effortlessly. Let us examine the novice procedure for tuning a lap steel guitar.

An extremely prevalent tuning for lap steel guitar is the open D tuning (D-A-D-F#-A-D), in which, when strummed freely, the strings are tuned to produce a D major chord.

Follow these methods to tune your lap steel guitar to open D tuning:

1. Beginning at D, tune the sixth string (which has the lowest frequency). As a guide, you may

utilize the reference pitch of a tuner or another instrument tuned to D.

2. Align the fifth string to an in-pitch of A, which corresponds to the fifth fret of the sixth string.

3. Align the pitch of the unbowed fourth string with the fourth fret of the fifth string, resulting in the fourth string tuned to D.

4. Align the intonation of the third string to F#, which corresponds to the fourth fret of the fourth string.

5. Align the second string with the fifth fret pitch of the fourth string, which is A.

6. At last, adjust the pitch of the first string to D, which corresponds to the open fourth string.

After achieving the desired frequencies on all six strings, verify the tuning by performing chords and individual notes while moving the fretboard. To ensure precision, employ an electronic tuner or tuning application, making any required modifications to align each string precisely.

The lap steel guitar is capable of revealing an infinite number of musical possibilities through experimentation with tunings. Investigate alternative tunings, such as open G and open C, or even custom tunings crafted to your artistic vision, as your proficiency grows.

It is critical to perform routine tuning inspections and maintenance on your lap steel guitar to ensure consistent intonation and sound quality. Establishing the practice of calibrating one's instrument before every performance or practice session is crucial for achieving maximum playability and musical expression. Through consistent effort and perseverance, the ability to tune your lap steel guitar will be ingrained as an instinctive capability, granting you the capability to investigate the acoustic possibilities of the instrument with assurance and simplicity.

## Engaging In Open Chords

Acquiring the skill of lap steel guitar can lead to a captivating exploration of slide guitar methodologies and the creation of mesmerizing, emotive music. It is essential, whether you are a complete novice or making the transition from another instrument, to grasp the fundamentals. An exhaustive manual elucidating three fundamental principles suitable for novices: the execution of open chords, the investigation of major and minor scales, and the introduction of slide techniques.

Many lap steel guitar melodies are constructed upon open chords. In contrast to the conventional method of fretting strings with the fingertips, lap steel guitarists apply tension to the strings using a steel bar. Tune the lap steel guitar to an open tuning, such as D-G-D-G-B-D, to commence. Once adjusted, perform open chords by following these steps:

1. Commence by establishing the D major chord. Position the steel bar at the second fret across all strings. Develop a luminous, resonant D major chord by strumming each string.

2. G Major: To execute the G major chord, raise the steel bar across all strings to the fifth fret. Strings up, except the low D string (the sixth), strumming will yield a robust G major chord.

3. A Major: To perform the A major chord, move the steel bar to the seventh fret. Strum every string except the low D string.

4. E Major: Position the steel bar at the ninth fret across all strings to form the E major chord. Strum every string to achieve a lively E major note.

5. Minor Chords: Flatten the third note of the major chord shape to perform minor chords.

For instance, compress the F# to F and strum all strings at the second fret to achieve D minor.

Strive to execute seamless transitions between these open chords, guaranteeing that every note resonates with clarity. Beginning gently, increase your pace progressively as your confidence grows.

## An Examination Of Major And Minor Scales

A comprehension of major and minor scales is imperative to engage in improvisation and compose melodies on the lap steel guitar. Describe how to investigate these scales:

1. Major Scale: Commence by executing the D major scale, as it harmonizes harmoniously with the lap steel guitar's open tuning. The notes comprising the D major scale are D, E, F#, G, A, B, and C#. Sequentially employ the steel bar to fret each note along the strings, commencing at the open position and ascending the fretboard.

2. A compressed third note distinguishes the D minor scale from the D major scale, to which it is structurally similar. The notes that constitute the D minor scale are D, E, F, G, A, Bb, and C. By honing this scale pattern across the fretboard, you should correspondingly modify the position of the steel bar.

Explore various rhythmic patterns and cadences to develop your musical expression as you play these scales.

## An Overview Of Slide Techniques

Slide techniques are essential components of lap steel guitar performance, facilitating the generation of graceful missions and emotive melodies. Listed below are some fundamental slide techniques for novices:

1. Single Note Slides: Commence by producing a continuous pitch by effortlessly sliding the steel bar across a solitary string. Develop your ability to slide the fretboard with precision and control.

2. Double stops are accomplished by synchronously dragging the steel rod across two adjacent strings. Explore various intervals, including thirds and fifths, to generate double-stop phrases that are harmonious.

3. Vibrato: Vibrato enhances the emotional profundity of your performance. To generate vibrato, maneuver the steel bar in a gentle oscillatory motion while ensuring consistent contact with the strings. Gain experience manipulating the vibrato's pace and intensity to achieve a variety of effects.

4. Slurs and bends entail the act of slurring or bending into notes that are pitched lower. To add expression to your performance, experiment with bowing strings upwards and downwards using the steel bar.

5. Investigate the technique of glissanding complete chord structures across the fretboard to generate dynamic chord progressions.

Concentrate on preserving precision and clarity while performing chord slides.

Regularly applying these slide techniques will help you develop fluidity and command of your instrument. As your proficiency increases, challenge yourself to integrate various techniques to produce a distinctive sound.

For novice lap steel guitarists, mastery of open chords, major and minor scales, and slide techniques constitutes the final pillar of the instrument. Allocate sufficient time to conscientiously practice each concept, and feel free to explore various tunings and musical genres to stimulate your creativity. Demonstrating perseverance, tolerance, and an unwavering enthusiasm for music will propel you forward on a gratifying quest to attain mastery as a lap steel guitarist.

# CHAPTER THREE

## The Integration Of Vibrato And Expression

The lap steel guitar is an enthralling musical instrument that imparts a distinctive essence to any composition. Learning lap steel guitar can be a rewarding experience for anyone, from seasoned professionals seeking to improve their abilities to complete novices anxious to explore the world of stringed instruments. This instructional manual will explore three essential elements of the lap steel guitar for novices: the integration of vibrato and expression, the acquisition of fundamental melodies and chords, and the comprehension of rhythm and timing.

Expression and vibrato are fundamental techniques that infuse vitality into the performance of lap steel guitar. The expressiveness and emotional impact of sustained notes are enhanced through the incorporation of a subtle wavering effect by vibrato. To enable vibrato in your performance, commence by positioning the slide, which is typically a tube made of glass or steel, over the desired string for vibration. Employing your plucking hand, maintain consistent pressure on the string while gently rocking the slide back and forth. Determine the optimal vibrato style by experimenting with its width and pace in the ambiance of the music.

Expression entails imbuing one's performance with musicality and expression through the use of dynamics, phrasing, and articulation. Investigate the effects of manipulating the intensity of the attack of your plucking hand to generate gentle, harmonious tones or forceful, aggressive accents. Concentrate on purposefully forming each note, incorporating slides, bends, and glissandos to imbue your phrases with vibrancy and complexity. Consider intricacies such as the depth and pace of your vibrato, in addition to the placement of rests and pauses, to generate tension and release in your performance.

It is advisable to pay close attention to seasoned lap steel guitarists to gain inspiration and direction. Analyze their methodologies and emulations of diverse musical genres, then integrate components that align with your musical inclinations. You will develop a distinctive lap steel guitar voice through perseverance and practice, one that is capable of communicating an extensive array of sentiments and musical expressions.

## Acquiring Fundamental Licks And Riffs

As a lap steel guitarist, learning fundamental melodies and chords is an excellent method to expand your repertoire and hone your abilities. As building elements for improvisation and soloing, licks are brief musical phrases or patterns; conversely, riffs are recurring motifs that define the personality of a composition or style. To commence, acquaint oneself with prevalent intervals and scales employed in lap steel guitar performance, including the major and minor pentatonic scales. Attempt to generate uncomplicated melodies and patterns utilizing these frameworks as inspiration.

By performing scales and exercises, one can improve their instrument dexterity and technique. It is essential to maintain a fluent motion and a relaxed posture while using both the selecting and gliding hands. Begin with brisk tempos and increase them progressively as your comfort with the material grows. Incorporate slides, bends, and vibrato into your lap steel guitar exercises to improve your expression and control.

Expand your musical vocabulary by delving into various genres and styles of music once you have achieved a sense of command over the fundamentals. Analyze the cadence, tone, and feel of legendary lap steel guitarists from a variety of musical genres, including Hawaiian, jazz, country, and blues. Engage in the exploration of integrating melodies and rhythms from these musical genres into your performance, modifying them to align with your musical inclinations and aesthetics.

## Comprehending Timing And Rhythm

Rhythm and timing are fundamental components of music, serving as the structural support for the construction of melodies and harmonies. Lap steel guitarists must develop a strong sense of timing and cadence to collaborate with other musicians and compose unified musical arrangements. Commence by engaging in fundamental rhythmic exercises and patterns, with an emphasis on sustaining a consistent pulse and internalizing various beat subdivisions.

Practice maintaining a consistent tempo and rhythm while playing along with a metronome or percussion machine. As your familiarity with the material grows, progressively escalate the complexity of the patterns from simple to more intricate. Demonstrate meticulousness in your cadence and diction, endeavoring to achieve exactitude and precision with each note you execute.

Explore and implement diverse rhythmic feels and accents to introduce variety and intrigue into your performance. It is advisable to engage in collaborative practice by playing along with recordings showcasing a diverse range of musical genres.

The primary objective should be to replicate the cadence and atmosphere of the music while also incorporating your imaginative embellishments. Cultivate your capacity to attentively perceive and react to the subtleties of the music, adapting your performance to harmonize with the collective ambiance and tonality of the ensemble.

One can significantly advance in their mastery of lap steel guitar playing by integrating vibrato and expression, acquiring fundamental melodies and chords, and developing an understanding of rhythm and timing. It is crucial to maintain a consistent practice routine, remain receptive to novel concepts and influences, and above all, derive pleasure from the boundless exploration of this multifaceted instrument.

## Utilizing Backing Tracks For Practice

When beginning to play lap steel guitar, the use of background recordings is an indispensable practice aid. Implementing your timing, cadence, and improvisational abilities, backing recordings provide a musical backdrop against which you can practice playing along with various styles and tempos.

To begin effectively utilizing accompaniment tracks, it is essential to locate tracks that correspond to one's musical preferences and level of expertise. Online platforms offer an extensive collection of accompaniment tracks, encompassing intricate arrangements as well as straightforward chord progressions, and diverse musical genres including jazz, country, blues, and Hawaiian. Explore various recordings to identify those that elicit a personal response and correspond to your present skill level.

After deciding on a backdrop track, begin by carefully listening to it to acquaint yourself with its chord progressions, melody, and overall atmosphere. Concentrate on the cadence and melody, as this will assist you in maintaining time with the song and guide your performance.

Commence your musical performance by executing basic melodies or improvising on top of the accompaniment track. Concentrate on maintaining time with the music while attentively observing how your performance works into the overall musical ambiance.

As your comfort level increases, introduce variety into your musical repertoire by attempting out distinct scales, techniques, and rhythmic patterns.

An advantageous aspect of utilizing accompaniment tracks for practice is that they offer an interactive and dynamic environment in which to refine one's abilities. Implement them to refine particular facets of your musical performance, including soloing, chord alterations, or dynamics. In addition, performing along with accompaniment recordings can better your aptitude and your versatility as a musician across various musical styles and keys.

Do not hesitate to experiment and make errors as you advance. Backing tracks provide a secure and encouraging setting in which to test out novel concepts and challenge one's musical capabilities.

Embrace the chance to acquire knowledge from your errors and utilize them as motivation for personal growth.

For novice lap steel guitarists, practicing with background recordings is, in conclusion, a beneficial resource. It provides opportunities for creative expression and experimentation in addition to an enjoyable and engaging method to develop your musical abilities. You can enhance your proficiency and develop into a more versatile and self-assured musician by integrating background recordings into your study regimen.

# CHAPTER FOUR

## An Overview Of Various Styles, Including Blues, Country, Hawaiian, And Others

Exploring the wide variety of musical genres that lap steel guitar can be employed to perform is among the most enthralling facets of learning the instrument. There is something for every individual to discover and appreciate, whether they are inclined towards the mesmerizing melodies of Hawaiian music, the soulful tones of blues, or the twangy tones of country music.

Blues music is distinguished by its improvisational style, emotive melodies, and expressive vocals. To imbue your lap steel guitar performance in the blues style with emotion and feeling, concentrate on employing techniques such as slide vibrato, bending, and gliding between notes. Conducting experiments utilizing various scales, including the pentatonic scale and the blues scale, will enable you to generate authentic blues noises.

Country music is renowned for its distinctive instrumentation, infectious melodies, and sincere lyricism. Since the genre's inception, lap steel guitar has been an integral part of country music, imparting a distinctive timbre and resonance to its sound. Plough steel on the lap in the country style by honing skills including double stops, open string riffs, and pedal steel bends. Gain knowledge of classic country melodies while attempting to imitate the cadence and manner of legendary lap steel players.

Hawaiian music, which is also referred to as "Hawaiian slack-key guitar," is widely recognized for its exquisite harmonies, intricate fingerpicking patterns, and lovely melodies. The lap steel guitar is inextricably linked with Hawaiian music due to its ability to generate the genre's signature fluid glissandos and rich overtones. The Hawaiian style of lap steel guitar requires mastery of techniques including slide slants, palm muting, and harmonics. Deepen your understanding of the intricate chord progressions and traditional tunings that comprise Hawaiian music, and fully engage with the abundant musical legacy that the islands possess.

Besides blues, country, and Hawaiian music, the lap steel guitar possesses the versatility to be adjusted to an extensive array of genres, such as jazz, rock, folk, and more. Explore diverse musical traditions and genres to uncover undiscovered tones and broaden your musical perspectives.

In general, acquiring the skill of lap steel guitar instruction provides an extensive array of musical opportunities, enabling one to investigate and appreciate a wide spectrum of styles and genres. Whether you are inclined towards the mesmerizing tones of Hawaiian music, the soulful sounds of blues, or the twangy tones of country music, this versatile instrument offers an extensive repertoire of possibilities.

## Suggestions For Enhancing Your Playing

1. Consistent Practice: Similar to any other musical instrument, lap steel guitar mastery requires consistent practice. Each day, allocate specific practice time to refine one's technique, repertoire, and musicality. Over time, even brief practice sessions can result in substantial progress.

2. Concentrate on Accuracy: Strive for precision in your performance while paying close attention to your intonation. Utilize a tuner to ensure that your guitar is in tune, and utilize accompaniment recordings or other instruments to practice playing in tune. Determine the optimal slide angle and finger

position for producing a consistent and accurate sound.

3. Construct Your Tone: Using various fingerpicking, slide, and picking techniques, experiment to determine which tone complements your musical style the most. Concentrate on generating a rich, silky tone with excellent sustain. Explore various techniques, including volume surges and palm muting, to enhance the dynamics and expressiveness of your performance.

4. Gain knowledge of music theory: A solid grasp of music theory can significantly augment one's artistic prowess and ingenuity. Apply what you have learned about scales, chords, and harmony to your lap steel guitar playing. Possessing knowledge of the fundamental principles of music will enable you to confidently improvise and make well-informed musical decisions.

5. Develop Your Repertoire: To increase your musical vocabulary, investigate a vast array of musical styles and genres. Adapt musical compositions from various eras and cultures to the lap steel guitar. Explore various tunings and techniques to develop a distinctive musical style.

## Preserving The Lap Steel Guitar

1. Regular Maintenance: After each playing session, sanitize your lap steel guitar by rubbing it down with a gentle, dry cloth. Prevent the accumulation of grime, grit, or fingerprints on the body, fretboard, and strings to preserve their optimal playability.

2. Regularly replacing your strings will ensure that they continue to be in tune and produce the finest possible sound. Utilize rubbing alcohol or string cleaner to eliminate debris and prolong the life of your strings. Inspect damaged strings for signs of deterioration or corrosion, and replace them without delay.

3. Humidity Management: Keep the environment surrounding your instrument at a constant level of humidity to avert deformation, splitting, and other forms of damage. Dehumidify or humidify as necessary to maintain relative humidity levels that fall within the instrument's specifications.

4. Lap steel guitars should be stored when not in use in a durable case or instrument bag to prevent dust, moisture, and accidental damage.

Strain from subjecting your guitar to direct sunlight or extreme temperatures, as doing so may result in harm to the finish and components.

5. Consistent Maintenance: Arrange routine maintenance inspections with a certified guitar technician to guarantee that your instrument remains in pristine condition for performing. Inspect and make any necessary adjustments to

the bridge, frets, and nut to preserve intonation and playability.

Novices can commence a gratifying expedition into the realm of lap steel guitar performance by adhering to the aforementioned tricks and strategies. You can generate aesthetically pleasing music for many years by harnessing the expressive capabilities of this one-of-a-kind instrument through diligence, perseverance, and a fervor for music.

## Conclusion

In summary, commencing the study of lap steel guitar as a novice can offer a transformative experience replete with musical revelation and individual development. It is essential to maintain perseverance, commitment, and a willingness to learn throughout this process.

Before beginning your lap steel guitar voyage, keep in mind the following fundamentals: familiarity with the instrument, its tuning, and fundamental techniques such as slide control and muting. Consistent practice is essential for developing muscle memory and a keen sense of intonation and tone.

Furthermore, investigate a multitude of beginner-friendly resources, such as instructional literature, online tutorials, and video lessons. These resources may offer you insightful advice, practical exercises, and suggestions that will facilitate your progress.

In addition, feel free to explore various playing styles, genres, and techniques to discover your distinctive sound on the instrument. By incorporating various musical genres into your practice, including blues, country, Hawaiian, and others, you will expand your musical horizons and improve your abilities.

Above all else, derive pleasure from learning and composing music on the lap steel guitar. Embrace obstacles as learning opportunities and commemorate your advancements throughout the process.

By exercising diligence, unwavering determination, and an insatiable enthusiasm for music, you will rapidly attain the ability to adeptly traverse the fretboard and articulate your thoughts effortlessly via the evocative tones of the lap steel guitar.

www.ingramcontent.com/pod-product-compliance
Lightning Source LLC
LaVergne TN
LVHW021442231224
799792LV00002B/290